Classical vs. Modern Education:

A Vision from C.S. Lewis

Stephen R. Turley, Ph.D.

TURLEY TALKS
A New Conservative Age Is Rising
www.TurleyTalks.com

www.TurleyTalks.com

Copyright © 2016 by Dr. Steve Turley. All Rights Reserved.

ISBN-13: 978-1978199194

ISBN-10: 1978199198

No part of this publication may be reproduced, stored in a retrieval system, or transmitted in any form or by any means, electronic, mechanical, photocopying, recording, scanning, or otherwise, except as permitted under Section 107 or 108 of the 1967 United States Copyright Act, without either the prior written permission of the author, or authorization through payment of the appropriate per-copy fee to the Copyright Clearance Center, Inc., 222 Rosewood Drive, Danvers, MA 01023, (978) 750-8400, or on the web at www.copyright.com. Requests to the author for permission should be addressed to steve@turleytalks.com.

Cover image credit: © 2012 Rob Shenk, Flickr | CC-BY-SA | via Wylio

Table of Contents

1. Waterfalls and the World

7

2. Classical Education and Culture

11

3. The Modern Revolution

15

4. The Abolition of Man

21

5. The Education Renaissance

27

Conclusion

31

Other Books

33

About TurleyTalks

35

About the Author

37

CHAPTER 1

Waterfalls and the World

There is no doubt that the 1940s constituted a most historically formidable decade: the Japanese attack on Pearl Harbor, WWII, the advent of the Atomic bomb, the transformation of the U.S. into a global super power, the establishment of NATO, the founding of the People's Republic of China. Yet among these notable events one rarely if ever comes across the inclusion of a small book, published in 1944, critiquing the state of British education. The book was entitled *The Abolition of Man*, and its author was one of the great literary minds of the twentieth-century, the renowned Oxford and Cambridge scholar, C.S. Lewis. In what is perhaps the single most significant analysis of the modern age published in the twentieth-century, Lewis in less than 100 pages outlines what Prof. Peter Kreeft calls a terrifying prophecy of mortality, not just the mortality of modern western civilization, but the mortality of human nature itself.

Lewis' critique was initiated by a textbook, which he leaves unnamed, calling it *The Green Book*, written by two authors he also leaves unnamed, referring to them as Gaius and Titius.

The authors of this book recount the famous visit to the Waterfalls of the Clyde in Scotland taken by the poet Samuel Taylor Coleridge in the early 1800s. As Coleridge stood before the waterfall, he overheard the response of two tourists: one remarked that the waterfall was "sublime" while the other said it was "pretty." Coleridge mentally endorsed the first judgment and rejected the second with disgust. Gaius and Titius then offer their own commentary on this scene:

> When the man said *That is sublime*, he appeared to be making a remark about the waterfall.... Actually ... he was not making a remark about the waterfall, but a remark about his own feelings. What he was saying was really *I have feelings associated in my mind with the word 'Sublime'*, or shortly, *I have sublime feelings* ... This confusion is continually present in language as we use it. We appear to be saying something very important about something: and actually we are only saying something about our own feelings.

For Lewis, this comment by Gaius and Titius had nothing less than cosmic consequences. The waterfall scene and the commentary captured in microcosmic fashion *two contrasting conceptions of the world*: one, represented by Samuel Taylor Coleridge, which affirmed beauty as an objective value embedded in a created cosmic order and recognized by a humanity that participates in that cosmic order; the other, represented by Gaius and Titius and the *Green Book*, which denied objective value in impersonal nature and located all conceptions of beauty and sublimity to the human mind and to personal preference. In the one, beauty is a value that exists independent of the knower; for the other, beauty is a value constructed by the knower and superimposed on an impersonal world. For Lewis, these two perspectives represent nothing less than *two fundamentally different human projects*, what can be considered two fundamentally different ages or civilizations, what we might call the *moral* age versus the *modern* age, the *sapient* versus the *scientific* age.

Lewis summarizes these two ages thusly: For classical man, the fundamental question was: "How do I conform my soul to the world around me and thus be drawn up into divine life?" The answer was through prayer, virtue, and knowledge. However, for modern man, the question is inverted: modern man is not interested in how to conform the soul to reality. Instead modern man asks, "How do I conform the world to my own desires and ambitions?" The answer involves tapping into those institutions that operate by the mechanisms of power and manipulation, namely, science, technology, and the state.

Now what Lewis observes with the *Green Book* is that these two contrasting visions of reality entail two contrasting visions of education. Perhaps one of the more profound observations that Lewis makes is that education is inescapably *enculturation*; education is a means by which one is initiated into a culture, into a particular way of being human. For Lewis, the significance of the *Green Book* as a textbook was that it marked the triumphant arrival of the modern age and its assumptions pervading British culture such that now all cultural institutions, most especially the schools, are reconstituted according to secular rules, understandings, and goals.

But Lewis is not merely a critic of this civilizational shift. He is not a cynical curmudgeon who simply laments the death of the old order and the rise of a new one. No, Lewis believes that this propensity, this orientation, toward power and manipulation inherent in the modernist experiment is nothing less than a threat to our humanity as we have known it.

Peter Kreeft, Professor of Philosophy at Boston College and The King's College, summarizes well Lewis' concern:

> [*The Abolition of Man*] is prophetic; it is couched in scholarly language, in fact its plethora of learned Latinate references scare away even college students today, for this is the first generation in American history that is less well educated than its parents, but its content is a terrifying prophecy of mortality, not just the mortality of modern western civilization ..... but the mortality of human nature itself if we do not recapture belief in [what Lewis calls] the *Tao*, the natural law, the doctrine of objective values.

CHAPTER 2

Classical Education and Culture

In order to understand where Lewis is coming from, we have to understand culture and education as they were understood for nearly 2,200 years in the Western world, from Plato to the mid-nineteenth-century. Education in the classical sense of the term was inextricably linked to what the Greeks called *paideia*. We use a similar term when we take our kids to a pediatrician. In the Greco-Roman world, *paideia* had a two-fold meaning. Originally it referred to the educational project of the Greeks to initiate a student into a culture, into a particular way of being human. But it eventually became synonymous with the actual content of that culture, and was thus the Greek counterpart to the Latin *cultura*. So, *paideia* is both the content of culture and the educational process by which one is initiated into culture; in short, the 'cultivation of culture.'

This conception of education became very important for the emerging Christian civilization. This is because of a key text in Ephesians 6:4, where St. Paul exhorts fathers to raise their children in the *paideia tou kyriou,* the "*paideia* of the Lord." Paul brings in this *paideia* idea, but this is not a *paideia* of the Greeks or the Romans; this is a *paideia* of the Lord. This is a *paideia* that is not of this world so it is bringing in a culture literally of another world, the world of heaven itself. And so you have Christians developing the Greco-Roman conception of *paideia* in strikingly new and unprecedented ways.

However, this of course raises the question: What is culture? Here we have to understand the classical relationship between *paideia* and the *polis* or the Greek city-state. The chief aim of the city-state was to bridge the gap between the individual human person and the larger macrocosmic world. We have to understand that in the classical world, there was a micro-macro relationship between the human person and the larger cosmic world. Empedocles in the fifth-century BC was not only the first to systematize the four elements of the cosmos, but also the four humours of the human body (yellow and black bile, phlegm and blood) that corresponded with each other in relationships analogous to the four cosmic elements. The human person was thus a microcosmic replication of the wider macrocosmic world that was filled with divine meaning and purpose.

This micro-macro relationship meant that every person born into the world is born into a world of divine obligation, so all people are obligated to orient their lives in a way that realizes the divine purpose for humanity. This is what classical scholars have called "cosmic piety," which was nearly universal in the Greco-Roman world. For the Greek, there was a profound sense that one was truly human only to the extent that one was in a harmonious relationship with the cosmos.

And so this is the context in which we need to understand *culture*: the culture or *paideia* of the city-state represented the reconstitution of time and space around this divine obligation and thus enabled us to fulfill our divine purpose and thereby become truly human. So whether you are dealing with history, art, literature, math, economics, music, science, etc, all of these constituents are tangible material expressions of this divine meaning and purpose which we embody and thereby orient our lives in accordance with cosmic virtue.

Now, when it came to education, this conception of culture as a materialized expression of cosmic piety was precisely that world into which a student was initiated. The goal was to bring about a harmony between the three aspects of the soul – the intellectual, moral, and emotional – which was demonstrated in an ethical life of civic virtue, the ideal citizen of the polis; the way Lewis puts it, the goal was to produce "men with chests." This is what the term "virtue" means: *vir* is the Latin term for "man."

So, by way of summary: classical education was a project by which the student was initiated into a culture that materialized or substantiated a cosmic piety that enabled the student to fulfill his divine purpose and thereby become truly human. And this vision of education remained normative for 2,200 years, beginning with Plato. It flourished under the Romans and then into Christendom, and all the way up to the mid-nineteenth-century.

CHAPTER 3

The Modern Revolution

Now, for Lewis, this classical conception of education and its various frames of reference was eclipsed by the rise of the modern age.

With the break-up of Christendom in the seventeenth-century, it became increasingly plausible to view knowledge as limited solely to that which could be verified by a *method*, namely, the application of science and reason. It was argued that only those things that could be verified by the empirical method were those things that could be known in a way that was completely detached from the preconceptions of the observer. Anything that was not subjected to or failed this method was reduced to the state of person-relativity and excluded from the arena of what can be known. Thus knowledge was now open to man: all he had to do, in any area of life, was to apply the method.

But there was a toll that had to be paid for such promise. One of the first victims of this new view of knowledge was cosmic piety: because divine meaning and purpose is impervious to the scientific method it cannot be known, and so it became increasingly plausible to see the world as comprised of cause and effect processes that have no meaning apart from that which people chose to give to it.

As a result of this new view of knowledge, you have a whole new definition of religion: religion is no longer a civilizational expression of cosmic piety; instead, religion is simply something that you personally believe but cannot know. Religion gives you personal meaning, but it has no public or objective value *at all*. And if religion cannot be known, then it never leaves the realm of doubt, and thus doubt is the proper orientation toward the church's claims.

With the rise of the scientific method as the sole way of knowing, the church is pushed completely from the public square, into the periphery of society, consigned solely to one's private life. And what this means is that each person born into this world is born into a world devoid of any divine obligation apart from that which you choose to impose upon yourself. It is therefore no coincidence that it was in the nineteenth and twentieth centuries that Christians began to stress a personal relationship with Jesus irrespective of the church. While classical Christianity simply lacked the frames of reference to bifurcate one's soul from culture, by the beginning of the twentieth-century, the public/private distinction imposed upon Christianity by secularized processes was firmly in place.

And with the marginalization of the church, our whole conception of culture has changed. The term *culture* today is used more in a social scientific sense which can be very misleading; this is because the fundamental assumption to this social scientific sense is that there is no inherent meaning or purpose that is objectively discernable in this world, and so meaning is specific to the human race. Humans by their nature impute meaning to an otherwise meaningless world. And this is the role of culture: *culture is composed of common symbols, practices, and arrangements shared among a distinct population by which they impute meaning to a meaningless world.* This is why we can never say that one culture is any more valid than another, since all cultures are by their nature arbitrary; they fabricate meaning systems that are artificial in relation to impersonal nature. Hence, we arrive at multiculturalism, the notion that all cultures are equally valid, which is another way of saying they are all equally artificial.

Now perhaps we can see why Lewis is so concerned with *The Green Book*. If education is always enculturation, then *The Green Book* represents nothing less than the attempt to enculturate students into the modern vision of the world. Modern education must *by definition* perpetuate and enculturate a dichotomy between science and religion, fact and faith, knowledge and belief. It must *by definition* turn students away from the classical vision of cosmic piety and cut them off from encountering the transcendent and eternal values of the True, the Good, and the Beautiful. Indeed, according to Gaius and Titius and the *Green Book*, Truth, Goodness, and Beauty are now whatever you want them to be. We are all now born into a world where we have no divine obligations whatsoever apart from that which we choose personally to impose upon ourselves.

But Lewis observes that if students are cut off from encountering the transcendent, then we have cut them off from the very source of civic virtue; we have cut them off from the cosmic values by which they might foster a balanced soul and thus become truly human. For example, Saint Augustine argues that virtue involves properly ordering our loves, or what he called *ordo amoris*. It is good to love a baby, and it is good to love a ham sandwich; but if both the baby and ham sandwich were falling off a ledge and I rush to save the ham sandwich, something is wrong with my loves. The order of my loves has been dislodged from the economy of goods that God has created.

And the danger here, which classical civilization recognized, is that without conforming itself to the cosmic values of Truth, Goodness, and Beauty, the human soul collapses into either an unethical rationalism or an unthinking sensualism. Thus, on the one hand, you have university professors like Peter Singer at Princeton who advocate infanticide (what he calls post-birth abortions) up to the age of two; on the other hand, we have today the radical pornification of pop culture. This is all totally predictable: in a modern age that cuts us off from the transcendent, our intelligentsia are going to be radically unethical and our pop-culture icons are going to be radically sensual.

And yet, as Lewis notes, 2,200 years of cultural and educational precedent doesn't go away overnight. It has a way of lingering in our consciences and our expectations. Thus, Lewis observes the strange irony that we in the modern age still expect these virtues to be operative in our society. We still expect honesty, courage, a commitment to the common good and human flourishing. And yet how can we do that? How can we teach our students that truth is relative and expect our politicians to be honest? How can we claim that morality has been replaced by situational ethics and expect Wall Street executives to ground their business decisions in anything other than profit, greed, and expediency? How can we think beauty is solely in the eye of the beholder and then complain how publicly funded art is so often offensive? How can we claim the classical family to be merely an arbitrary western cultural construct and still repopulate the planet? How can we amputate university dorm-life from the medieval conception of solitude and contemplation and prevent them from turning into brothels that house students, some of whom will be our future medical and bio-ethicists? And how can we consider Christianity as merely one of innumerable Oprah-ized alternatives for personal fulfillment and meaning and still value the sanctity of human life?

Lewis puts it this way:

> And all the time – such is the tragic-comedy of our situation – we continue to clamour for those very qualities we are rendering impossible. You can hardly open a periodical without coming across the statement that what our civilization needs is more 'drive', or dynamism, or self-sacrifice, or 'creativity'. In a sort of ghastly simplicity we remove the organ and demand the function. We make men without chests and expect of them virtue and enterprise. We laugh at honour and are shocked to find traitors in our midst. We castrate and bid the geldings be fruitful.

CHAPTER 4

The Abolition of Man

Now, what are the consequences of this? What happens if we do not change course? What happens if education continues to be value-neutral, as it were, cutting off students from an encounter with the transcendent?

Lewis recognizes that if all values are relegated to the person-relative, if all conceptions of Truth, Goodness, and Beauty are collapsed into the subjective as personal preferences, then the only way there can be a moral consensus in society is through the use of coercion. If a sense of divine obligation and hence self-government has been erased, then only coercion, compulsion, and extortion can provide a motivation for ethical conformity.

This is not very difficult for us to imagine. I am sure most of you have either read the books or seen the movies of the *Lord of the Rings* trilogy by Lewis' colleague J.R.R. Tolkien. There is a wonderful scene in the movie *The Two Towers* when Frodo, who is travelling through Middle Earth to get rid of an evil ring in the fires of Mordor and facing countless life-threatening adversities along the way, looks at his companion Samwise Gamgee and just begins to despair, saying: "I can't do this Sam." Sam responds:

> I know. It's all wrong. By rights we shouldn't even be here. But we are. It's like in the great stories, Mr. Frodo. The ones that really mattered. Full of darkness and danger, they were. And sometimes you didn't want to know the end. Because how could the end be happy? How could the world go back to the way it was when so much bad had happened? But in the end, it's only a passing thing, this shadow. Even darkness must pass. A new day will come. And when the sun shines it will shine out the clearer. Those were the stories that stayed with you. That meant something, even if you were too small to understand why. But I think, Mr. Frodo, I do understand. I know now. Folk in those stories had lots of chances of turning back, only they didn't. They kept going. Because they were holding on to something.

"What are we holding on to Sam?" Frodo asks. "That there's some good in this world, Mr. Frodo," Sam responds with determination, "and it's worth fighting for."

Now, can you imagine how different Sam Gamgee's response would be had he been educated with *The Green Book*? What would be the only way you could have gotten Frodo and Sam to make the sacrifice to travel across Middle Earth at the expense of life and limb, sacrificing everything on behalf of their Shire that doesn't even know what is going on? Well one way would be to kidnap their families and hold them ransom,

"You do this or else"; this is called *consequentialism.* Another way would be to offer them a great reward. Either way, a world educated on the *Green Book* cannot say: "You should do this because it is good!" Those enculturated through the *Green Book* would say: "There's nothing objective about goodness; it's just a matter of opinion!" Or, "Goodness is merely in the eye of the beholder!" And if morality and ethics fall outside the realm of knowledge, then we have lost all objective frames of reference by which to agree on what is right and wrong. And if there is no objective basis for ethical conformity, then the only way we can have any kind of mass ethical conformity is through some institution that has the power to compel such conformity. Thus, Lewis sees manipulation at the heart of this brave new world to which we are embarking.

This propensity to manipulation is part of modernity's larger project which puts forward a new *summum bonum,* a new greatest good, which is man's conquest of nature. You will recall Lewis' observation above: classical man was interested in conforming the wants and needs of the human person to the world around him, while modern man is interested in conforming the world to the wants and needs of the human person. *It really is all about you* as the advertisement confidently declares. If there is no divine meaning or purpose in nature, if it is only cause and effect processes that have no inherent meaning or purpose apart from what we choose to impart to it, then nature is simply there to be used according to our purposes.

Now, if manipulation is an intrinsic characteristic of modern life, then, Lewis observes, you must by definition have two classes of people: manipulators and manipulatees, or, in Lewis' terms, the "conditioners" and the "conditioned." The need for coercion and manipulation thus gives rise to the formation of a social elite, a secular aristocracy.

So why would the masses agree to this new social arrangement? Why would they ever volunteer to be ruled by an elite class of manipulators? Simply put, because the masses have been conditioned to believe that life and happiness are found when we conform the world to our own desires and ambitions. But such promise requires our trusting dependence upon a class of elites who have the expertise to so conform the world. The elites promise life without limit, health in perpetuity, psychological wholeness and wellness, the protection of group rights and bodies, unlimited educational and career opportunities and prosperity for all. *The genius of this new modern division of labor is the success it has had in enslaving the masses by convincing them that the extent to which they are dependent on social engineers is the measure of their freedom.* The modern experiment has successfully convinced mass populations that control over nature is the new *summum bonum,* and the more we rely on social engineers to provide such control over nature, the freer we will become. For example, it is not mere coincidence that the name of the card the state of Maryland issues to access public food and cash assistance is the "Independence Card." Our freedom is contingent on the extent to which we are dependent on social engineers comprised of scientific, technological and statist elites.

And here is Lewis' chilling conclusion: If nature is by definition that which is to be conquered and controlled, that which is to be conformed to my needs and desires and ambitions, and if this view of nature involves a control and manipulation of people as the only way of bringing about moral conformity, then this project of man's conquest over nature means that the vast majority of the human population has to be consigned to the category of nature. We are being manipulated right along with the natural world! Thus, man's conquering of nature includes man's conquering of himself, or, better, the use of nature for the power of some over others. Our attempt to conquer nature has given nature the last laugh. Nature has conquered us.

Lewis gives the obvious example of contraception, where those who control nature in effect control other humans. This is precisely the driving force behind abortion, and why today you have a class of elites that sees abortion as more sacred than the Second Amendment: abortion, unlike the Second Amendment, *controls nature and thus embodies the greatest good.* This is what is behind the manipulation and redistribution of wealth by social engineers. The vast majority of the population is "nature" and is there to be controlled and manipulated in accordance with the goals and desires of the manipulators.

Lewis writes:

> We have been trying, like Lear, to have it both ways: to lay down our human prerogative and yet at the same time to retain it. It is impossible. Either we are rational spirit obliged for ever to obey the absolute values of the *Tao* [Lewis' word for the doctrine of objective values], or else we are mere nature to be kneaded and cut into new shapes for the pleasures of masters who must, by hypothesis, have no motive but their own 'natural' impulses. Only the *Tao* provides a common human law of action which can over-arch rulers and ruled alike. A

dogmatic belief in objective value is necessary to the very idea of a rule which is not tyranny or an obedience which is not slavery.

Hence, by attempting to conform the world around the self, we end up incarcerating ourselves. Modern culture becomes a kind of prison that surrounds us, absorbs and distracts us, and cuts us off from the transcendent values that bring balance to the soul and awaken the liberty inherent in civic and moral virtue. Thus, Lewis concludes that modern education, to the extent that it perpetuates this religion vs. science dichotomy, enculturates students into a world constituted by conditioners and the conditioned, a new social order that subsumes the vast majority of humanity under the category of impersonal nature which in effect redefines humanity as inherently meaningless; hence the title of his book, the *Abolition of Man*.

CHAPTER 5

The Education Renaissance

Now, in the midst of all this, what should we do? Should we climb into our bunkers and despair, or is there any reason for optimism?

The good news is that in the last three decades we have seen nothing less than a renaissance of classical Christian education in our nation, in the rise of classical schools, homeschooling, and confessional colleges and universities. According to the Association of Classical Christian Schools membership statistics, there were 10 classical schools in the nation in 1994, today there are over 230. Since 2002, student enrollment in classical schools has doubled from 17,000 nationwide to 35,000, and all indicators suggest that the next decade will be one of significant growth. And we are already seeing the effects of this kind of education. Classical schools in 2011 had the highest SAT scores in each of the three categories of Reading, Math, and Writing among all independent, religious and public schools.

And the secular world is taking notice. Take for example the recent article on Tall Oaks Classical School in *Delaware Today* by the editor-in-chief: "Does Delaware Have a Blind Spot in the Education Arena? The success story of Tall Oaks' classical learning style cannot be ignored." The main article goes on to show how churches, working together through the teachers and students at Tall Oaks, are renewing and redeeming education in ways that secular schools could never hope to do.

Homeschooling has also grown astronomically in the last three decades. In 2003, there were an estimated 2,100,000 children homeschooled nationwide, which grew to 2,500,000 in 2009, representing an average growth rate of 7-15% per year. According to the National Center of Educational Statistics, the percentage of all school-aged children homeschooled in the U.S. increased from 1.7% in 1999 to 3% in 2009, representing a 74% increase over a ten-year period.

The school choice movement is stronger than ever. As of June 2015, 18 states and the District of Columbia offered private school choice programs. Nearly a quarter of million students nationwide are participating in either voucher programs or tax-credit programs. The former governor of Louisiana, Bobby Jindal, pursued perhaps the most significant program of school privatization, where he shifted tens of millions of dollars from the public school monopoly to pay for private, and mostly Christian, schools.

In 2010, the widely-acclaimed documentary *Waiting for Superman* exposed a significantly large audience to how modern public education is collapsing under the weight of the teachers' unions. In fact, *Waiting for Superman* was written and directed by Davis Guggenheim, producer of the Al Gore environmental film, *An Inconvenient Truth*, so it is hardly an example of right-wing propaganda. And another documentary, *Indoctrination,* does a very good job of tracing out the history of the modern public education monopoly in the US and its agenda of creating willing participants in the current secular statist project.

We therefore have many reasons to be very optimistic.

So what can you do? What is your role in all of this?

First, if you are currently a parent of a school-age child, I respectfully urge you to think deeply and soberly about these two visions of education and which one is compatible with the kind of culture into which you want your children initiated. The good news is that there is no shortage of educational opportunities that foster classical civic virtue in your children. There is a literal classical education renaissance going on right now, and so there is no shortage of educational venues for you to take advantage of.

The second thing is that if you are not a parent with a school aged child, if you're a grandparent or your kids have grown up, one of the best things you can do is set up a scholarship fund through one of the schools or at a church or some kind of trust, so that families who are strapped for cash can have a way of participating in this recovery of classical education. Obviously the chief impediment of taking advantage of classical education is cost, and so there are a lot of families who could really use financial help, and setting up some kind of scholarship fund would be a magnificent contribution to the recovery of civic virtue in our society.

The Green Book by Gaius and Titius would have us believe that the purpose of education is to make men subservient to the goals and habits of the modern age, masters of method, guardians of utilitarianism and pragmatism, equipped to deconstruct human nature and cultural endeavor as empty social constructs. Standing against these dehumanizing tendencies is the nineteenth-century English art critic John Ruskin's description of the purpose of education. Ruskin writes:

> The entire object of true education is to make people not merely do the right things, but enjoy the right things — not merely industrious, but to love industry — not merely learned, but to love knowledge — not merely pure, but to love purity — not merely just, but to hunger and thirst after justice.

If we are to see a restoration of civic virtue in our society, we must take seriously the reformation of the institutions that educate the next generations. We must once again restore the frames of reference that secure the transcendent nature of the True, the Good, and the Beautiful in this world, and thus foster within our children hearts of virtue and a sanctified moral imagination that seeks the common good and human flourishing in all. In so doing, the next generations will grow up knowing that there is indeed good in this world, and it is worth fighting for.

Conclusion

Thank you again for purchasing this book!

I hope this book helped you to understand and appreciate the profound difference between classical and contemporary education.

As I encouraged you above, the next step is to get involved with a classical education association that can direct you to a local classical school, provide resources for starting your own, or provide resources and support for classical homeschooling. Here's a list of some organizations and associations that you can get involved with:

- The Association of Classical & Christian Schools: https://classicalchristian.org/
- The Society for Classical Learning: https://societyforclassicallearning.org/
- The CiRCE Institute: https://www.circeinstitute.org/
- Scholé Academy: http://www.classicaleducator.com/
- Classical Conservations: https://www.classicalconversations.com/

Finally, if you enjoyed this book, then I'd like to ask you for a favor. Would you be kind enough to leave a review for this book on Amazon? I'd greatly appreciate it!

Thank you so much, and may God richly bless you!

Steve Turley
www.turleytalks.com

Check Out My Other Books

Below you'll find some of my other popular books that are popular on Amazon. Simply go to the links below to check them out. Alternatively, you can visit my author page on Amazon to see my other works.

Awakening Wonder: A Classical Guide to Truth, Goodness, and Beauty
https://www.amazon.com/Awakening-Wonder-Classical-Goodness-Education/dp/1600512658/

Worldview Guide for A Christmas Carol
https://www.amazon.com/Worldview-Guide-Christmas-Classics-Literature/dp/1944503862/

Stressed Out: Learn How an Ancient Christian Practice Can Relieve Stress and Overcome Anxiety
https://www.amazon.com/Stressed-Out-Christian-Practice-management-ebook/dp/B076GDQZMC

The Ritualized Revelation of the Messianic Age: Washings and Meals in Galatians and 1 Corinthians
https://www.amazon.com/Ritualized-Revelation-Messianic-Age-Corinthians/dp/056766385X/

If the links do not work, for whatever reason, you can simply search for these titles on the Amazon website to find them.

About www.TurleyTalks.com

Are we seeing the revitalization of Christian civilization?

For decades, the world has been dominated by a process known as globalization, an economic and political system that hollows out and erodes a culture's traditions, customs, and religions, all the while conditioning populations to rely on the expertise of a tiny class of technocrats for every aspect of their social and economic lives.

Until now.

All over the world, there's been a massive blowback against the anti-cultural processes of globalization and its secular aristocracy. From Russia to Europe and now in the U.S., citizens are rising up and reasserting their religion, culture, and nation as mechanisms of resistance against the dehumanizing tendencies of secularism and globalism.

And it's just the beginning.

The secular world is at its brink, and a new traditionalist age is rising.

Join me each week as we examine these worldwide trends, discover answers to today's toughest challenges, and together learn to live in the present in light of even better things to come.

So hop on over to www.TurleyTalks.com and have a look around. Make sure to sign-up for our weekly Email Newsletter where you'll get lots of free giveaways, private Q&As, and tons of great content. Check out our YouTube channel (www.youtube.com/c/DrSteveTurley) where you'll understand current events in light of conservative trends to help you flourish in your personal and professional life. And of course, 'Like' us on Facebook and follow us on Twitter.

Thank you so much for your support and for your part in this cultural renewal.

About the Author

Steve Turley (PhD, Durham University) is an internationally recognized scholar, speaker, and classical guitarist. He is the author of *Awakening Wonder: A Classical Guide to Truth, Goodness, and Beauty* (Classical Academic Press) and *The Ritualized Revelation of the Messianic Age: Washings and Meals in Galatians and 1 Corinthians* (T&T Clark). Steve blogs on the church, society and culture, education, and the arts at TurleyTalks.com. He is a faculty member at Tall Oaks Classical School in Bear, DE, where he teaches Theology, Greek, and Rhetoric, and Professor of Fine Arts at Eastern University. Steve lectures at universities, conferences, and churches throughout the U.S. and abroad. His research and writings have appeared in such journals as *Christianity and Literature, Calvin Theological Journal, First Things, Touchstone*, and *The Chesterton Review*. He and his wife, Akiko, have four children and live in Newark, DE, where they together enjoy fishing, gardening, and watching *Duck Dynasty* marathons.

Made in the USA
Middletown, DE
27 September 2019